CONTENTS

WHO WE ARE

The Apache peoples have lived in the areas that are now Arizona, New Mexico, and Texas for at least the last 1,000 years. In the Apache language, they call themselves *Ind'e* or *Nde*, which mean "people." The Apache language is part of the **Athabascan** language family. The Apache share this language family and ancestors with the Diné, or Navajo, and other Indigenous peoples.

Apache children enjoy horse riding at a rodeo in the Fort Apache Indian Reservation in Arizona.

The Sunrise Ceremony is a celebration that marks a girl's growth into womanhood.

Think!

Many cultures around the world have coming-of-age ceremonies such as a *bat mitzvah* or a *quinceañera*. Why do you think this is?

The word *Apache* has its roots in the Spanish and Zuni languages. The term means "outlaw or enemy." But the Apache peoples widely use this name as well.

The Apache are a **matrilineal** people. To the Apache, becoming a warrior is a **sacred** calling. Men and women have been warriors. This calling can occur at a very young age. The training and ceremonies that go into becoming a warrior can be intense.

The Apache are known for their strength and resilience. They keep their culture and way of life alive. They honor their ancestors. They honor the land that gives them food to live. They honor the bison, or buffalo, as a symbol of the hunt and of knowledge. They are connected to the land in all directions.

OUR LIVES TODAY

Today, 13 different Apache nations live in the United States. The White Mountain Apache **Reservation** is the largest reservation for the Apache nations. It includes 1.6 million acres (648,000 hectares) of land. The San Carlos Apache Tribe has the largest population. It has 16,000 **enrolled** members.

Apache citizens can be found in all professions and across the United States and beyond. Some serve in the military, some are artists, some are lawyers, some are leaders, and some are teachers. Many work to help their nation and their people.

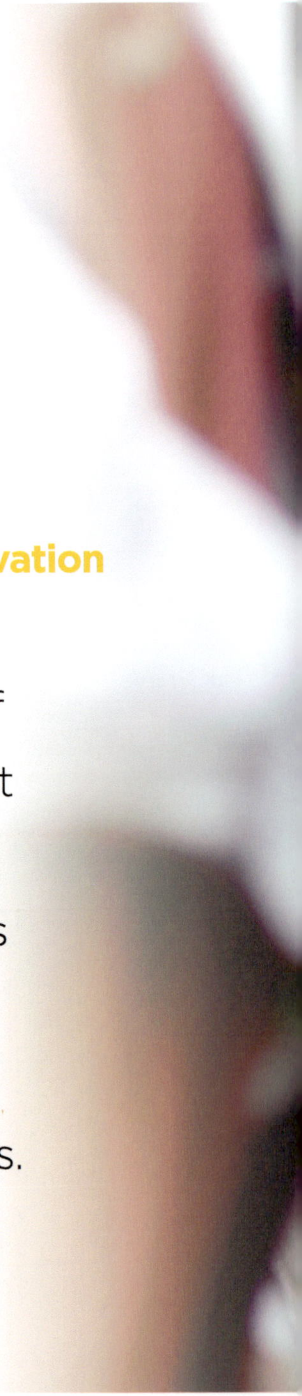

George Mornel, Apache veteran of the Vietnam War

Tammie Allen is a Jicarilla Apache potter. She works with a special clay found in the mountains of New Mexico.

Dr. Sylvestor A. Moses serves his San Carlos Apache community in the hospital on their tribal land. He is working to bring more Apaches into

Students from Jicarilla Apache Nation and Sangre de Cristo School explore Apache pottery.

the medical field. He believes that Apaches healing Apaches is important to their community.

Josef Sanchez was an engineer at the National Aeronautics and Space Administration (NASA). After NASA, he became Vice President of Space Systems at Hyperspace Technologies, Inc.

Aurelia Bullis is an Apache language teacher. She works to preserve and pass down the Apache language. She was also hired to bring **authentic** Apache dialogue to the movie *Horizon: An American Saga*.

Ask Questions!

What questions do you have about Apache life today? Work with an adult to help you find answers.

Sierra Blanca, in New Mexico, is one of four mountains sacred to the Apache. It is located on the Mescalero Apache Indian Reservation.

Make a Guess!

Why are mountains important to Apache peoples? Make a guess, then research to find out if you were right.

OUR ANCESTRAL LANDS

The Apache peoples hold the land as sacred. They have a spiritual and cultural connection to it.

Traditionally, the Apache lived high in the mountains, within valleys, in deep canyons, and in the desert. These areas included Eastern Arizona, Northern Mexico, New Mexico, West Texas, and southern Colorado. These places were called Apacheria.

The Apache were **nomadic**. They relied on the land to provide food. They traveled with the seasons and hunted bison. They built **wickiups** out of young trees, grass, and bark. For them, the land isn't just something that they live on. It is something they live in community with.

Recreation of a historic Apache camp and wickiup at Fort Bowie National Historic Site

The United States forced Indigenous peoples onto reservations during **Indian Removal**. The Apache nations resisted fiercely. Geronimo was an Apache warrior and **medicine man**. He led raids against the United States military for years. Geronimo stood as a figure of Indigenous resistance. He was forced to surrender in 1886.

Eventually, Apache nations were settled on reservations. But the reservation system did not end their connection to the land. They still fight to protect it.

Apache land is rich with natural resources. It is often under attack by those who want to strip it of those resources. Oak Flat is a sacred site in Arizona. But companies want to mine the copper there. Mining would destroy the site. **Advocates** have introduced bills in Congress and filed court cases to protect it.

An Apache activist protests to save Oak Flat from copper mining.

DO NOT
SACRED LAND
ENTER

CARRYING TRADITIONS FORWARD

In any tribal nation, religious beliefs and traditions vary. The Apache nations are no different. Each may have their own ceremonies and belief system that are unique to them. Apache peoples continue those traditions today in many ways. Apache crown dancers are one example. They represent mountain spirits during ceremonies. Traditions like this honor the past, present, and future of their people.

Create!

With an adult, go online and find out what kinds of classes and workshops an Apache nation hosts. Create a flyer advertising one of the upcoming events.

Another tradition welcomes military veterans home with a special ceremony. Kristopher Killsfirst is a U.S. Army veteran. He received the ceremony when he returned from his service. A song was made for him by his father-in-law. It is still sung today. Veterans know their community honors their service.

Elders continue to teach traditional hunting and harvesting of important Apache foods like agave. Apache hunters carried dried strips of agave with them on hunts. Agave is also important in ceremonies such as the Sunrise Ceremony.

Today, Apache peoples still practice their beliefs. They teach them to their children. They build a future of their own making.

Twila Cassadore leads a foraging and hunting trip to share Apache knowledge of traditional foodways.

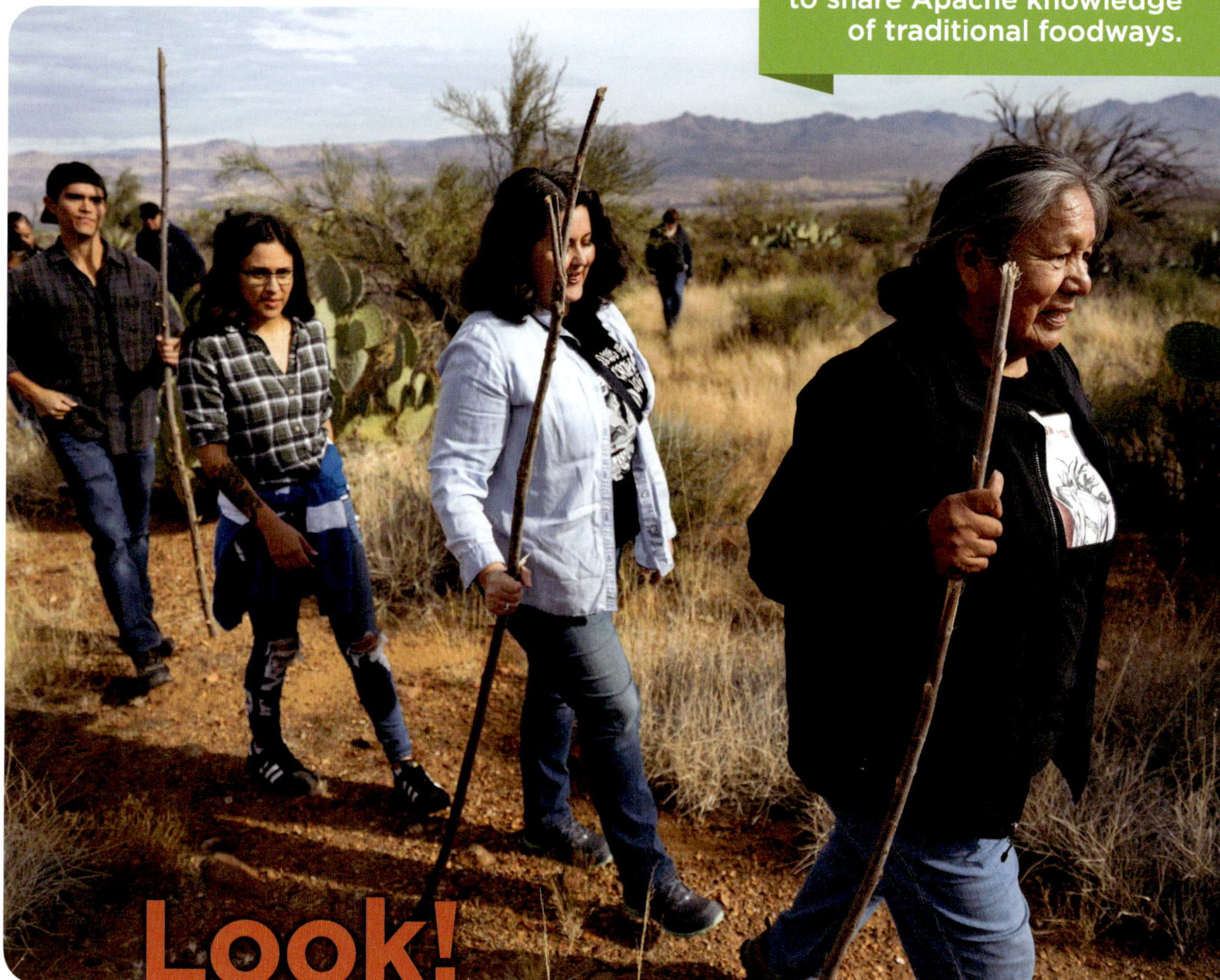

Look!

What do you notice about the land in the image? What does that tell you about traditional Apache life?

GLOSSARY

advocates (AD-vuh-kuhts) supporters who work for a cause or to advance a policy

authentic (uh-THEN-tik) honest and true

Athabascan (aa-thuh-BAA-skin) belonging to a cultural and language family that includes Indigenous peoples from Alaska, Canada, coastal California and Oregon, and the U.S. Southwest

enrolled (in-ROHLD) officially belonging

Indian Removal (IN-dee-uhn rih-MOO-vuhl) law signed in 1830 that forced Indigenous peoples off their lands

matrilineal (maa-truh-LIH-nee-uhl) a society structured through the mother's family

medicine man (MEH-dih-suhn MAN) an honored member of Indigenous communities who helps heal the sick and often provides holy guidance

nomadic (noh-MAD-ik) a lifestyle where a person or group of people move around frequently and do not have permanent settlements

sacred (SAY-kruhd) holy; important to a system of belief

wickiups (WIH-kee-uhps) dome-shaped Apache homes were made from grass, animal hides, and other materials

FIND OUT MORE

Books

Bruegl, Heather. *Diné.* Ann Arbor, MI: Cherry Lake Press, 2025.

Michaels, Sarah. *Geronimo for Kids: The Warrior Who Wouldn't Give Up.* Anaheim, CA: BookStem, 2024.

Thiele, June. *Geronimo.* Ann Arbor, MI: Cherry Lake Press, 2023.

Online

With an adult, explore more online with this suggested search.

- Jicarilla Apache facts for kids | Kiddle

Say Hello!

Dagotee (dah-goh-tay) — a Western Apache greeting that means "How are you?"

Da'anzho (dah-ahn-zho) — an Eastern Apache greeting that means "How are you?"

INDEX

ABOUT THE AUTHOR

Heather Bruegl, a member of the Oneida Nation of Wisconsin/Stockbridge-Munsee, is a Madonna University graduate with a Master of Arts in U.S. History. She is a public historian and decolonial educator, and her Munsee name is Kiishookunkwe, meaning "Sunflower in Full Bloom." Heather frequently travels to present on Indigenous history, policy, and activism, bringing her deep knowledge and personal connection to the subject.